WRITING A HUMAN RESOURCES MANUAL

Susan Brock

Sally Cabbell

CRISP PUBLICATIONS, INC.
Los Altos, California

WRITING A HUMAN RESOURCES MANUAL

Susan Brock
Sally Cabbell

CREDITS
Editor: **Marian Jane Sanders**
Designer: **Carol Harris**
Typesetting: **Interface Studio**
Cover Design: **Carol Harris**
Artwork: **Ralph Mapson**

Copyright © 1989 by Crisp Publications, Inc.
Printed in the United States of America

Crisp books are distributed in Canada by Reid Publishing, Ltd., P.O. Box 7267, Oakville, Ontario, Canada L6J 6L6.

In Australia by Career Builders, P.O. Box 1051 Springwood, Brisbane, Queensland, Australia 4127.

And in New Zealand by Career Builders, P.O. Box 571, Manurewa, New Zealand.

Library of Congress Catalog Card Number 88-72250
Brock, Susan; Cabbell, Sally
Writing a Human Resources Manual
ISBN 0-931961-70-X

PREFACE

A Human Resources Manual (also called an Employee Handbook) is a must-have for every business. Regardless of company size, employees need to know certain organizational policies, practices, and procedures. If you don't yet have an HR Manual, you need one. If you already have one, you may need to update it. *WRITING A HUMAN RESOURCES MANUAL* responds to either need.

Providing information to employees is more than just being helpful. Some policies, such as equal employment opportunity and harassment, are mandatory. Other policies, such as employee conduct standards and expense policies, clarify an organization's practices; they help the employee fit in and adjust to the company's climate.

As you go through this book, you'll have a chance to develop or update your own HR Manual. The exercises and examples will help you tailor the information to your company's needs. By the time you finish this book, you'll have a comprehensive outline on which to base your organization's own manual.

After your manual is set up, keep this book handy as a reference. Employees will appreciate knowing important personnel policies, and supervisors will appreciate having a source to support them when they have to enforce those policies.

Good Luck!

Susan Brock

Sally Cabbell

ABOUT THIS BOOK

WRITING A HUMAN RESOURCES MANUAL is not a book to read; it's a book to use. The unique self-paced format of the book encourages you to get involved and to try some new ideas immediately.

This book introduces you to both the philosophy behind developing a Human Resources (HR) Manual and the practical step-by-step approach to writing it. Go through this book with a pencil in hand, so you can jot ideas in the margins and complete the exercises with your company in mind.

By the time you finish, you'll have a comprehensive outline that will form the basis for your own manual. You'll also know the difference between an HR Manual and a Policy Manual. When you finish, keep this book around—it will be a handy reference for periodically updating your manual.

CONTENTS

PREFACE   i

PART 1—WHAT IS A HUMAN RESOURCES MANUAL?
Differences Between the *HR Manual* and the *Policy Manual*   2
Why Do You Need an HR Manual?   5
What Will this Book do for You?   6

PART 2—HOW DO YOU KNOW WHAT TO TELL YOUR EMPLOYEES?
How Do You Know What to Tell Your Employees?   8
Finding Out What You Need to Say   9
Using the Checklist as an Interviewing Tool   10
Interviewing the Managers   12
Using the Checklist as a Table of Contents   13
Thinking Through the Policies   14

PART 3—WRITING POLICY SUMMARIES
Sample Statements for a Policy Manual   18
Sample Statements for an HR Manual   22
How to Write a Policy Summary   23
About Style   24
    Exercise #1: Writing for Clarity   27
    Exercise #2: What's Wrong with this Policy Summary   29
    Exercise #3: Test Your Knowledge!   33
Testing and Verifying the Contents   42

PART 4—USING YOUR HUMAN RESOURCES MANUAL
Using Your Human Resources Manual   44

PART 5—REVIEW
Can We Help You?   46
Summary of Worksteps   47
Updating Your HR Manual   48

APPENDIX
Subjects to Consider: Mandatory, Important, & Nice-To-Have   50
Sample Table of Contents for a Policy Manual   53
Sample Tables of Contents for Two HR Manuals   55
Sample HR Manual—XYLON Company   57

PART 1

WHAT IS A HUMAN RESOURCES MANUAL?

DIFFERENCES BETWEEN THE HUMAN RESOURCES (HR) MANUAL AND THE POLICY MANUAL

Before you begin, some background information may be useful. First, your organization already has policies and procedures, although they may not be written in a formal document. Your company's unwritten personnel practices *are* policies; policies that will hold up in a court of law. It is therefore a good idea to have your practices and precedents documented the way *you* want them to be interpreted—not the way the courts might interpret them.

This formal document is called a *Policy Manual* (or a *Policies and Procedures Manual*). The Policy Manual includes detailed descriptions or explanations of personnel policies, company rules, or employee benefits. The HR Manual (or Employee Handbook) contains a synopsis of these detailed policies. The HR Manual may also state a company rule or explain an employee benefit, but the information is more concise, and the language is usually more casual. Although this book includes information on the Policy Manual, its primary purpose is to explain how to put together an HR Manual.

Two examples of the same personnel policy, one from an HR Manual and one from a Policy Manual, are shown on the facing page.

EXAMPLE FROM AN HR MANUAL

[This example of a policy summary is typical of those found in HR Manuals.]

EMPLOYEE DEVELOPMENT SECTION

Tuition Reimbursement

We encourage you to improve your education and skills. Under special circumstances, you may be reimbursed for the tuition cost of educational courses taken outside normal working hours. Should you desire to participate in such a program, consult with the Human Resources Department for details of the policy and for a Tuition Reimbursement form.

EXAMPLE FROM A POLICY MANUAL

[This example shows how comprehensive the information in a Policy Manual is.]

SECTION 600: EMPLOYEE TRAINING AND DEVELOPMENT

XYLON COMPANY

Subject: **TUITION REIMBURSEMENT**	Policy No.: 602. Page 1 of 2 Date: May 21, 19XX

I. PURPOSE

To encourage employees to improve their skills and job knowledge and to enhance their opportunities with the company.

II. POLICY

The company will often assist employees to improve their job skills by reimbursing them for a portion of the tuition costs of approved job-related academic courses which they wish to take on their own time.

(CONTINUED NEXT PAGE)

EXAMPLE FROM A POLICY MANUAL (continued)

III. ELIGIBILITY AND CONDITIONS

A. This policy applies to regular, full-time employees with six months or more of continuous service.

B. Eighty percent of the cost for tuition will be reimbursed upon successful completion of the course.

C. Approval must be requested prior to course registration and should include an estimate of the time and expense involved. Requests for approval should be submitted to the appropriate supervisor or department head. Copy of approval form is attached.

D. Courses must be job-related and will be considered for approval on a course-by-course basis even though they may be part of a Certificate or Degree program.

E. Reimbursement will be made upon satisfactory completion of the course and upon presenting receipts indicating the actual cost incurred.

F. The cost of books, parking, and other fees will not be reimbursed.

XYLON COMPANY

Tuition Reimbursement

APPLICATION (To be submitted prior to course enrollment.)

Employee Name _____ Position _____ Date _____

Department _____ Course Title _____

Where will it be offered? _____ Date Completed _____

Hours of attendance _____ Tuition Cost _____

Approvals _____ _____
                           Supervisor   Human Resources

REQUEST FOR REIMBURSEMENT

I have completed the above course and wish to apply for tuition reimbursement. The following documentation is attached:

- Evidence of satisfactory completion.
- Copy of paid invoice covering tuition cost.

_____ _____
                  Signature   Date

Approvals _____ _____
                           Supervisor   Human Resources

INSTRUCTIONS

1. Complete application portion of form and submit to supervisor for approval prior to course enrollment.
2. Upon approval, return one copy to employee and retain one copy for personnel file pending course completion.
3. When course is completed, sign statement requesting tuition reimbursement, attach documentation, and submit to supervisor for processing.

You can see from reviewing these examples that the complete explanation of a policy as stated in the Policy Manual can be considerably shortened when you write the policy summary for the HR Manual.

WHY DO YOU NEED
AN HR MANUAL?

Now let's consider *your* objectives. You can clarify your goals by completing the sentence below—remember to be specific:

"After learning the concepts in this book, I want to write my own Human Resources Manual because: _____

_____

_____ ."

Need some help? Listed below are a few reasons that companies use HR Manuals. Check the boxes next to the reasons that apply to you and your company:

☐ There have been misunderstandings in our company that we need to resolve.

☐ We have lost good employees because of misinterpretations of company policies.

☐ Employees have filed complaints or lawsuits against the company because critical employee issues were not handled properly.

☐ The manner in which supervisors handle employee problems differs from one department to another.

☐ We need to verify that the information in our existing manual is the most appropriate for our organization.

If you checked any of the above boxes, your company needs an HR Manual!

The HR Manual explains important personnel policies in language that's clear and jargon-free. It can be used:

- by itself as a handy reference for all employees.

- with the employee bulletin board to communicate important news.

- as a management tool that "frees the hands of supervisors" by answering employees' questions.

WHAT WILL THIS BOOK DO FOR YOU?

After reading and practicing the ideas in this book you'll be able to:

- better understand why your company needs an up-to-date employee handbook,

- organize a clear and concise manual,

- select the required federal and state policies, as well as other important and useful policies that apply to your company, and

- keep your manual updated by referring to this book regularly.

TIP: If you want to correct and update your existing HR Manual, place your manual alongside this book and freely write notes in the margins of both books, so you can more easily change yours. If you want to develop an HR Manual for your firm, place a notepad alongside this book and jot down ideas as you read this book; then you can tailor the information to your organization.

HOW DO YOU KNOW
WHAT TO TELL
YOUR EMPLOYEES?

HOW DO YOU KNOW WHAT TO TELL YOUR EMPLOYEES?

A principal reason for developing an HR Manual is to clarify your company's organizational climate. Your manual tells employees what the company expects of them by the company and, in turn, what they can expect from the company. It clearly defines how the company wants to operate philosophically and functionally. Samples of setting the tone philosophically are:

> "We are a union-free manufacturer of widgits. We are proud of our ability to deal directly with our employees as one united team. We don't believe we need a third party to communicate for us, and we'll strive to keep this position."

> *or*

> "We are a fee-for-service organization. We are dedicated to delivering to our clients the highest quality service in our industry. In addition, we will operate conservatively to keep our clients' fees as fair and competitive as we can."

Many HR Manuals begin with a brief letter from the company president or chief executive officer. This letter can serve several purposes, including greeting new employees as they begin their first day of work or establishing the company philosophy (as in the previous examples).

A description of the company's background may follow the president's letter, but the bulk of the HR Manual will be a brief description or explanation of the policies and procedures that employees need to know. (The "Checklist for Organizations" on page 10 provides an outline of subjects often contained in HR Manuals.)

If you're uncertain what topics to include in your HR Manual, the remainder of this chapter will help explain.

FINDING OUT WHAT YOU NEED TO SAY

Ask the Managers!

Explaining how the company operates functionally is another goal of the HR Manual. One of the best ways to find out what information you need to include in your company's employee handbook is to ask the people who supervise and interact with employees daily: the supervisors and managers. By talking to the people who manage employees, you can tailor a generic checklist for an HR Manual (see next page) to meet your company's needs as perceived by its managers.

For example, if employees interact regularly with the public, you may want to define what the company considers appropriate behavior and attire when dealing with the public. Or if managers often encounter employees arriving late to work, you'll want to state the office hours and the company's policy and procedure for ensuring punctuality.

In the next few pages, you'll learn what subjects to consider when interviewing employee managers.

AS MANAGERS OF THIS ORGANIZATION, WE
NEED YOUR INPUT FOR OUR NEW HR MANUAL

USING THE CHECKLIST
AS AN INTERVIEWING TOOL

Generally, HR manuals will include the following subjects. (Subjects marked
''M'' are federally mandated for most employers.) Cross out the subjects that do
not apply to your company, and add subjects you think managers would want to
include. Your revised checklist will guide you not only in interviewing managers,
but in setting up a Table of Contents for your manual.

CHECKLIST FOR ORGANIZATIONS

1. Welcome Message from the Chief Executive
- ☐ Non-union statement
- ☐ Employment-at-will declaration (a statement that this manual doesn't constitute a contract guaranteeing length of employment)

2. Description of the Business
- ☐ Company philosophy; mission; or operating style
- ☐ History
- ☐ Products or Services
- ☐ Organization

3. Equal Employment Opportunity/Affirmative Action
- Ⓜ Equal Employment Opportunity (EEO) statement

4. Employment
- ☐ Employee status (full-time, part-time, etc.)
- Ⓜ Hours of work, rest, and lunch breaks
- Ⓜ Time tracking
- ☐ Personnel records
- ☐ Promotions and transfers
- ☐ Training programs
- ☐ Separation procedures

5. Wages and Salaries
- ☐ Wage and salary policy/philosophy
- ☐ Salary increase reviews
- ☐ Paydays
- ☐ Advances
- ☐ Overtime
- ☐ Deductions
- ☐ Automatic bank deposit

6. Safety and Health
- Ⓜ Safety rules
- Ⓜ Emergency procedures
- ☐ Medical services
- ☐ Safety organization
- ☐ Return to work
- ☐ Drug-free workplace

CHECKLIST FOR ORGANIZATIONS
(continued)

7. Company Standards and Rules
- ☐ Employee conduct
- ☐ Penalties
- ☐ Absence/tardiness reporting
- ☐ Telephone use
- ☐ Contributions and solicitations
- ☐ Wage attachments
- ☒ Sexual harassment

8. Legislated Employee Benefits
- ☒ Worker's compensation
- ☒ FICA (Social Security)
- ☒ Unemployment compensation
- ☒ Military duty
- ☒ Pregnancy leave of absence
- ☒ Time off to vote
- ☒ Jury duty
- ☐ (other state's legislated benefits)

9. Insured Employee Benefits
- ☐ Group health insurance
- ☐ Life insurance
- ☐ Long-term disability insurance
- ☐ Short-term disability insurance

10. Voluntary Employee Benefits
- ☐ Vacations
- ☐ Holidays
- ☐ Stock purchase
- ☐ Savings plan
- ☐ Credit union
- ☐ Retirement plan
- ☐ Tuition reimbursement
- ☐ Leaves of absence
- ☐ Sick pay
- ☐ Death in family
- ☐ Cafeteria/lunchroom
- ☐ Profit-sharing
- ☐ Severance pay
- ☐ Special privileges

11. Employee Relations
- ☐ Performance appraisal
- ☒ Complaint handling
- ☐ Bulletin boards
- ☐ Suggestion system
- ☐ Employee newsletter
- ☐ Employee recreation and social activities

If you're unsure which of the preceding subjects apply to your organization, the next few pages will show you how to select and develop the subjects that are most important for your company to include in its HR manual. To help you get started, consider the following:

- Which subjects do managers and supervisors complain about most often?
- Which subjects do employees ask about most often?
- Which subjects are currently least understood?
- Which employee work habits are most troublesome in the company?
- Are there state regulations defining subjects that need to be included?

State and Federal regulations change frequently.
Check your list carefully to see if you have included them all.

INTERVIEWING THE MANAGERS

Before you interview managers, complete the following steps:

1. Retype the checklist on the previous pages and include your additions and deletions.
2. Have all employee managers read a copy of the checklist, adding and deleting whatever subjects they choose.

With the managers reviewing and adding to the checklist, your manual will answer the questions most frequently asked by your employees.

3. Set up an appointment with each manager for a 30–45 minute interview. When you interview managers, review the revised checklist with them. As you go over the list together, ask them the following questions and take notes to record their answers:

- What are your major and/or most frequent employee problems?
- What subjects do your employees ask questions about over and over again?
- Which company policies are least understood by employees?
- Which employee benefits or privileges are most frequently asked about?

By asking the same questions of all managers, you will become better informed of the most useful subjects to include in your HR manaual.

USING THE CHECKLIST AS A TABLE OF CONTENTS

You can also use the checklist as if it were a table of contents. *First*, add all subjects suggested by the managers, as well as any subjects you believe will satisfy the concerns expressed in your interviews.

Second, review this table of contents with your boss and revise as needed. When you both agree on the content, you will have accomplished one of the toughest chores in developing an HR manual. Congratulations!

THE BEST APPROACH TO INTERVIEW A MANAGER IS TO FOLLOW A PREPARED LIST OF QUESTIONS.

THINKING THROUGH THE POLICIES

Once you've determined which policies to include, here's a good three-step approach to preparing the information for the one or two paragraph synopsis explaining each policy:

1. Ask both managers and employees as many questions as you can think of regarding the subject.
2. Formulate what you think the answers are and write them down.
3. Take the questions and answers to the policy decision-maker in your organization for confirmation of the answers.

This approach helps you to thoroughly think through the subject before your handbook makes any promises to the employees. A misstatement could be interpreted as a promise that the company may not want to keep.

For example, Jim Andrews, a human resources director at Xylon Company, wants to include in the HR Manual a policy that encourages employees to continue formal education. Here are some of the questions Jim needs to consider, so he can begin to establish guidelines:

- Should we pay for any type of college course taken?
- Should we pay for any courses the employee fails?
- Should we pay for tuition only? Or include books and lab fees?
- Should we pay for correspondence courses from a technical school?

Guidelines for a formal, detailed policy such as this one should be spelled out in your Policy Manual. (On page xx you saw an example of a Policy Manual's statement regarding tuition reimbursement.) Once you have carefully thought through your policy, you can summarize the important information in your HR Manual in a paragraph or two similar to the following:

> We encourage you to pursue a higher level of education that will enhance your abilities to perform your current jobs and prepare you for positions of greater responsibility.
>
> Upon successful completion of a job-related course taken onsite at an accredited college or university, Xylon Company will reimburse you for money spent on tuition, fees, and books. Ask you supervisor for forms and further details.

THINKING THROUGH THE POLICIES (continued)

These statements give employees enough information to know the company's position on educational benefits. Employees don't want to be burdened with too many details, but they need to know that more information is available in the Policy Manual if they want to pursue the subject.

Exception: You'll find that some subjects don't need a formal Policy Manual statement; a simple statement in the HR Manual will do. For example,

Xylon company sponsors a community softball team that competes in a corporate league. All employees interested in participating should contact Jim Andrews in the Human Resources Department. We are always looking for players, support crew members, and enthusiastic fans to cheer from the bleachers.

PART 3

WRITING POLICY SUMMARIES

Now that you've selected the subjects for your HR Manual, you can begin to write about them. First, though, let's look again at the differences between the detailed policies developed in a Policy Manual and the summarized policies found in an HR Manual.

SAMPLE STATEMENTS FOR A POLICY MANUAL

On the following pages are two statements from a Policy Manual: one on leaves of absence without pay and one on promotions. Note how comprehensively these policies are explained.

After your review, turn to page 22 and see how we've summarized these same policies for the HR Manual. As you develop your HR Manual, you will be preparing summaries of the detailed personnel policies found in your Policy Manual. If you don't have a Policy Manual, you may want to develop one to support your HR Manual.

---

[1]See page 50 in the Appendix for another list of subjects to consider as you begin developing your manual. This list organizes topics that are Mandatory, Important, or Nice-To-Have. As with the checklist in Part II, you'll want to include only those topics important to your company.

SAMPLE 1

XYLON COMPANY POLICY AND PROCEDURES MANUAL	Policy No. 304
	Date: January 11, 19XX
	Revised: _____
LEAVES OF ABSENCE WITHOUT PAY	Page 1 of 2

I. **PURPOSE**

To enable employees to receive extended time away from work to recover from medical disability, or handle pressing personal obligations.

II. **SCOPE**

This policy applies to all full-time Xylon Company employees.

III. **DEFINITION**

"Leave of absence" is defined as an excused absence without pay beyond ten working days. An absence involving paid time off (i.e., jury duty, sick leave, or funeral leave) is not considered a leave of absence.

IV. **POLICY**

Leaves of absence without pay may be granted to full-time employees to maintain continuity of service in instances where unusual or unavoidable circumstances require prolonged absence. (See IV, *Definition*, page 2.)

No loss of service credit with the company will occur as a result of the leave of absence, but no benefit credit will be accrued toward vacation and sick leave for the duration of the leave.

A. *Medical Leave.* An employee who has used all time available under the disability leave of absence policy (222.1) may request additional medical leave when supported by a physician's statement. Accrued sick leave benefits must be used prior to commencement of the leave. Therefore, medical leave will begin at the expiration of the period for which any benefit payment is made under the sick leave plan.

B. *Personal Leave of Absence.* A personal leave of absence to handle pressing personal obligations may be granted to full-time employees. Length of a personal leave of absence may range from 10–60 consecutive calendar days. To be eligible, the employee must have maintained a satisfactory record of employment with the company for a minimum of one year.

SAMPLE 1 (continued)

Leaves of Absence Without Pay, Continued

Approval of a personal leave of absence is made at the discretion of the employee's immediate supervisor with the concurrence of the Department Head. Although personal leave is a privilege, not a right, leave is usually granted, provided the employee's absence will not excessively disrupt the unit's operations. The employee must be available to return to regular employment on or before the expiration date of the leave.

V. **PROCEDURE**

A. *Application and Commencement*

Requests for leave of absence or an extension thereof must be submitted in writing to the supervisor ten days prior to the commencement date, except when medical conditions make such a requirement impossible.

B. *Reinstatement*

1. No guarantee of job availability can be made for employees returning from a leave of absence.

2. When possible, upon return from leave of absence, employees will be reinstated in the following priority of position reassignment:

    • First: prior position, if available.
    • Next: an equivalent position for which the employee is qualified, if available.
    • Next: a lesser position for which the employee is qualified.

    If no work is available according to the reassignment priorities listed above, the employee will be placed on inactive status and will be offered reinstatement if and when the first suitable position becomes available. If not reinstated, or, if the employee refuses an offer of a position, an employee's inactive status will terminate 12 months following end of leave of absence.

3. Employees on leave of absence must notify their supervisor at least two weeks prior to end of leave to inform the company of availability for return to work.

4. The company may require employees to have a physical examination to determine fitness for work prior to return from a leave of absence.

5. The company will consider an employee's failure to return from leave of absence, or present convincing reasons for not returning as arranged, as a voluntary quit.

SAMPLE 2

XYLON COMPANY POLICY AND PROCEDURES MANUAL	Policy No. 604
	Date: January 17, 19XX
	Revised _____
PROMOTIONS	Page 1 of 2

I. PURPOSE

To provide support to the basic organization-building process of promoting qualified employees to positions of greater responsibility and recognition.

II. SCOPE

This policy applies to all full-time positions.

III. POLICY

A. When a personnel vacancy occurs, all opportunities to promote from within will be explored consistent with the goal of filling positions with the most qualified individual available.

B. All full-time positions are posted consistent with the Job Posting Policy No. 631. Employees who are interested in applying for posted positions should follow the procedure outlined on the vacancy notice.

C. Supervisors may identify an employee for a promotion to an open position after discussion with and approval by the Department Head(s).

D. Performance Appraisals and other job related performance data will be reviewed when considering an employee for promotion.

E. A promoted employee maintains no rights to the previous position. If a job performance in the new position is unsatisfactory, or if the employee is otherwise dissatisfied, the employee may use the internal posting system to apply for another open position for which he or she is qualified.

F. At times, external recruiting sources will be used simultaneously with the internal search.

IV. RELATED POLICIES

POLICY NO. REFERENCES
Policy No. 601 *Employee Orientation and Training*
Policy No. 603 *Performance Appraisal*
Policy No. 631 *Job Posting*

SAMPLE STATEMENTS FOR AN HR MANUAL

The samples below are suggested summaries of the Leave of Absence without Pay Policy and the Promotion Policy illustrated on the preceding pages. Compare these summaries with the comprehensive policies, and note the difference in clarity and conciseness.

Sample –1—Leave of Absence Without Pay for Full-time Employees

When unavoidable situations arise where you need to take extended time off from work, the company may permit leaves of absence without pay. For example, a Medical Leave of Absence may be granted if you use all available disability time and sick leave but still need time to recuperate. A Personal Leave of Absence may be granted if you need time off to handle urgent personal obligations. A Leave of Absence Without Pay is for more than 10 days.

Except for medical emergencies, you must submit a written request for a Leave of Absence Without Pay to your supervisor 10 days in advance. The company cannot guarantee job reinstatement when you are ready to return, but we will attempt to return you to your prior position or another similar position. See your supervisor for additional details on this policy.

Sample –2—Promotions

Because our goal is to provide career enhancement for our employees, we will attempt to fill available positions by promoting from within. Supervisors may recommend qualified employees for available positions. We also encourage you to regularly check the Job Postings Bulletin Board and apply for positions of interest to you. Your qualifications for the position, as well as past performance noted on your performance appraisals, will be the major factors used to determine your eligibility.

Now that you've reviewed examples of detailed policy statements from a Policy Manual and compared them to summaries of an HR Manual, you're ready for your next step: writing your own policy summaries for your HR Manual. You're on your way now!

HOW TO WRITE A POLICY SUMMARY

The previous section showed the transformation from the detailed policies in a Policy Manual to the summaries in an HR Manual. By following these steps, you can create your own summaries:

1. Read the entire policy, as stated in your Policy Manual.

2. In your own words, simply summarize *aloud* what the policy says. Stating the policy aloud will help you express it conversationally.

3. Write what you said.

4. Check your written summary against the Policy Manual Statement to make sure you didn't omit anything important. If you don't have a Policy Manual, you will want to expand your HR Manual summary to include as many details as necessary to state your intent. If your HR Manual statements get too long, it's time to write a formal Policy Manual.

5. Now check your written summary again to make sure you didn't change the Policy's meaning. Although it's often helpful to use simple and clear language, you'll need to critically evaluate the accuracy of what you've said versus what you meant. And that means you'll need to clearly understand the comprehensive policy before you attempt to summarize it.

Although these five steps will help ensure that you've written a clear and concise summary, it's wise to add another step for additional verification. Page 42 provides additional information on Testing and Verifying the Contents of your policy summaries.

FIVE STEPS TO SUCCESS

ABOUT STYLE

Employee Handbooks sometimes suffer the same problems as business writing in general: too often they're stuffy, formal, and boring. A major complaint of human resources managers is that employees don't read important information distributed to them. And it's no wonder! Much of it isn't particularly readable.

Instead of concentrating only on content when you develop your HR Manual, consider packaging it to encourage your employees to read it. After all, the most carefully thought-out manual won't be effective if your employees put it in their desk drawers without reading it.

Several years ago, one company developed its HR Manual in a comic book format. At first managers were skeptical of the idea, but employees not only read and understood company policies, they actually practiced them—for the first time. By taking a typically dry, uninteresting document and packaging it to encourage employees to read it, the human resources department succeeded in accomplishing a goal of all companies: conveying the organizational philosophy, procedures, and policies in a way that people will understand and practice.

Of course, you'll need to consider your budget in developing your HR Manual. But many interesting approaches can be developed by thinking creatively rather than by spending a lot of money.

Format and design—use of subheads, bullets, lots of white space, illustrations, and cartoons—will make your manual readable and interesting. The sample HR Manual on the facing page shows how using artwork can make a page more interesting then having straight text only.

FRIENDLY SAMPLE PAGE

SAMPLE PAGE FROM HR MANUAL

HEALTH CARE BENEFITS

Your Xylon Company health care benefits have been designed to:

- protect you and your family against the financial burden of a major illness or injury;
- encourage preventive health care; and
- help you pay for necessary dental and vision care

The **MEDICAL PLAN** pays up to $1 million in lifetime expenses for you and each of your enrolled dependents, covering most of the cost of medically necessary care after you meet the plan's deductibles.

The **DENTAL PLAN** emphasizes preventive care by paying 100% of the cost of exams and cleanings once every six months. It also covers a good portion of the routine and major dental care you or your dependents need (after a deductible), and provides for up to $1,000 in lifetime orthodontia benefits for each of you.

The **VISION CARE** expenses are covered at 80%, and you pay no deductible. The plan pays for eye exams, prescription lenses, and frames once every 24 months.

This section of your handbook details many of the health care benefits provided through the Xylon Company plan. Information about how to claim your benefits is included in the Claims Guide section of your handbook.

Should you have additional questions, you can contact the insurance company, your local Employee Relations Department, or the Corporate Director of Employee Relations for more information.

GENERAL ORGANIZATION FOR YOUR MANUAL

A good approach to organizing information is to present it in this order:

1. Good news
2. Tough stuff
3. Upbeat finish

In other words, begin positively by letting employees know how highly the company regards them and by orienting them to the company's history or philosophy. Next, because most policies contain a Standards of Conduct section, try to phrase rules by using neutral or positive language rather than punitive language. For example:

BEFORE: It is a violation of company policy for employees to engage in dangerous horseplay. Violations of this rule are grounds for immediate disciplinary action, including termination.

AFTER: Because everyone should work in the safest environment possible, we expect employees to act professionally and not behave in a way that would endanger the well-being of others.

Last, finish your HR Manual with a paragraph or two promoting goodwill. Here's your chance to show your employees just how valuable they are to your company. You can say something such as: "We have done a good job in the past in this area and thanks to our mutual concern for safety, we know our efforts toward a safe working environment will continue to be positive."

EXERCISE #1:
WRITING FOR CLARITY

As you summarize company policies for your HR Manual, you'll want to write clearly, simply, and conversationally. This exercise provides practice in doing just that. Following are sentences that are wordy or unclear. Rewrite each sentence to make it concise and clear. When you're finished, check your answers with the authors' suggestions on the following page.

1. Due to the fact that most of our clients expect us to be here during normal working hours, in the majority of instances each and every employee is expected to be here between the hours of 8:00 a.m. and 5:00 p.m.

2. At this point in time, no provisions have been made to ensure that an employee's previous employment position will remain available in the event the employee returns to work after taking a leave of absence without pay.

3. It is the policy of this company to proceed in every given case to carefully and thoroughly interview each and every new job applicant to ensure that we maintain our standards of quality control.

"YOU TRY IT!"

SUGGESTED SOLUTIONS
FOR EXERCISE #1

1. **BEFORE:** Due to the fact that most of our clients expect us to be here during normal working hours, in the majority of instances each and every employee is expected to be here between the hours of 8:00 a.m. and 5:00 p.m.

> **AFTER:** Because we need to be as responsive as possible to our clients, we expect employees to be here during normal working hours—
> 8:00 a.m. to 5:00 p.m.

2. **BEFORE:** At this point in time, no provisions have been made to ensure that an employee's previous employment position will remain available in the event the employee returns to work after taking a leave of absence without pay.

> **AFTER:** If you take an extended leave of absence, we cannot guarantee that your prior job will be available when you return.

3. **BEFORE:** It is the policy of this company to proceed in every given case to carefully and thoroughly interview each and every new job applicant to ensure that we maintain our standards of quality control.

> **AFTER:** This company carefully interviews job applicants in order to hire those candidates best suited to the job.

EXERCISE #2:
WHAT'S WRONG
WITH THIS POLICY SUMMARY?

Here's your chance to identify weaknesses in the language and content of policies. Remember: policies should be clear, concise, and readable. That is, they should not contain technical jargon to obscure meaning or imply promises you may not want to keep. Your writing should express what you want to say rather than impress your reader with your command of the language. Check your answers with the authors' suggestions on page 32.

EXAMPLE—What's Wrong With This Policy Summary?

''Employees receiving written warnings of unacceptable performance or work habits must demonstrate improvement within 90 days or be terminated.''

This language could trap the company into keeping an unacceptable employee or paying wages for 90 days because the wording constitutes a 90-day guarantee of employment. Let's see how rewording this policy clarified it:

''Employees receiving written warnings of unacceptable performance or work habits must begin to demonstrate improvement immediately. Failure to demonstrate satisfactory improvement or progress may result in termination.''

By choosing words carefully, the rewritten policy doesn't commit the company to retaining unsatisfactory employees for a specified length of time. This frees the hands of management to operate in the best interest of good performers and the business in general.

EXERCISE #2:
WHAT'S WRONG WITH THIS
POLICY SUMMARY? (continued)

Now it's your turn! Each of the following three policies suffers from a weakness in policywriting. Read each carefully, identify the weakness, and rewrite the policy to make it more effective. Then, turn the page to check your responses with the authors' suggestions.

1. SAFETY GLASSES
Our manufacturing process could occasionally result in small particles of steel being projected through the air. These particles could pose a problem if they entered your eyes. Therefore, the Company provides safety glasses for your protection. We urge you to comply with OSHA regulations and wear your safety glasses at all times while on the factory floor.

Weakness: _____

Rewrite: _____

_____

_____

_____

2. SMOKING IN THE WORKPLACE
ABC Company wishes to comply with applicable health codes as well as to accommodate the wishes of both smokers and nonsmokers as much as possible without interfering with personal rights and the conduct of good business. Therefore, if a problem arises relative to smoking problems, management will try all reasonable methods to resolve the issue. If the issue is still not resolved to the satisfaction of both employees, the nonsmoking employee will prevail.

Weakness: _____

Rewrite: _____

_____

_____

_____

EXERCISE #2:
WHAT'S WRONG (continued)

3. EMPLOYEE REFERENCE CHECKS

Requests for information from employee files received from other departments for information on persons outside the organization will be directed to the Personnel Department where only date of hire, job title, and current employment status will be released. If the requesting party desires more information, the request must be in writing. A copy of the request and the reply will be kept in the employee's personnel file.

Weakness: _____

Rewrite: _____

_____

_____

_____

WATCH FOR PITFALLS AS
YOU PREPARE POLICY SUMMARIES

SUGGESTED SOLUTIONS
FOR EXERCISE #2

SAFETY GLASSES

1. Weakness: Wishy-washy safety policy

Suggested Solution: Our manufacturing process requires cutting, forming, and assembling parts of cold rolled steel. Metal particles from these processes can fly through the air at any time. Therefore, safety glasses, both clear lens and prescription, will be provided for your protection everywhere in the manufacturing and warehouse areas. Failure to wear your safety glasses will result in discipline and possible discharge.

SMOKING IN THE WORKPLACE

2. Weakness: Vague/confusing policy

Suggested Solution: ABC Company respects the individual preferences of smoking and nonsmoking employees. When these preferences conflict, we anticipate that most instances will be resolved through mutual courtesy and cooperation. If, however, a conflict arises and is not resolved, the manager and Director of Personnel will assist the employees in reaching an agreement. If no satisfactory solution can be found, the area will be designated a nonsmoking area and signs will be posted to that effect.

EMPLOYEE REFERENCE CHECKS

3. Weakness: Policy creates a company liability

Suggested Solution: No one in the ABC Company is permitted to release any information on any employee except the designated member of the Human Resources Department to whom the employee has given a written Release of Information form.

If you know someone will be calling or writing for reference information about you, ask your supervisor or anyone in the Human Resources Department for a Release of Information form. Complete this form by designating the facts you will allow to be released and signing and dating the form. Send or deliver the form to the Human Resources Department. This Release will be valid for a maximum of 30 days.

EXERCISE #3:
TEST YOUR KNOWLEDGE!

How did you do with the previous exercises? Are you ready for the big test? By now you probably better understand the differences between detailed policies and policy summaries. Here's your chance to test your newly acquired knowledge.

On the following pages are three comprehensive policy statements. Read each carefully, then write a policy summary in the spaces provided below. When you finish, turn to page 41 and check your answers with the authors' suggestions.

1. Overtime: Non-exempt Employees

2. Personnel Records and Privacy

3. Performance Appraisal

EXERCISE #3:
TEST YOUR KNOWLEDGE!
(continued)

Subject: **OVERTIME:** **NON-EXEMPT EMPLOYEES**	Policy No.: 202 Page 1 of 2 Date: May 21, 19XX

I. PURPOSE
To provide guidelines for the administration of overtime pay policy.

II. POLICY
The company overtime pay policy will conform to overtime provisions of the Federal Fair Labor Standards Act and the California State Industrial Welfare Commission Wage Order. Exemption from these provisions shall be claimed for an employee only when it can clearly be established that the employee's duties and responsibilities meet all requirements for such exemption.

The overtime pay policy for employees includes the following principal elements:

1. Non-exempt employees will be paid straight time for hours worked—up to eight in one day and forty in one week.

2. Non-exempt employees will be paid time-and-one-half for hours worked— in excess of eight in one day or forty in one week.

Policy No.: 202
Page 2 of 2

OVERTIME, continued

3. Non-exempt employees will be paid double time for hours worked:

   a. In excess of 12 in one day.
   b. In excess of eight on a seventh consecutive work day in any one week.
   c. On company holidays.

4. Paid time off for holidays, jury duty, bereavement leave, and vacation is considered to be ''hours worked'' for overtime calculation purposes. Paid sick leave and other leaves without pay will not be considered ''hours worked.''

5. All overtime worked by non-exempt employees must be authorized in advance by the supervisor or department head.

6. When overtime is incurred, non-exempt employees will be paid as described above rather than granted compensatory time off.

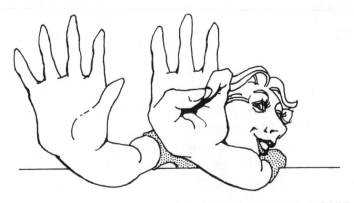

TIME AND ONE HALF FOR OVER EIGHT HOURS

EXERCISE #3: (continued)

XYLON COMPANY

Subject:	Policy No.: 204
PERSONNEL RECORDS & PRIVACY	Page 1 of 2
	Date: May 21, 19XX

I. **PURPOSE**

To maintain a standard by which documents and information contained in personnel records will be managed and processed.

II. **POLICY**

Employee records maintained by the company will contain only information that is relevant and necessary to meet various legal requirements and to assure efficient personnel administration. They will be managed to assure accuracy and protect employee privacy.

III. **PROCEDURE**

A. *Personnel Record*

A file for each employee, containing the information listed below, is maintained in a confidential and secure manner under the custodianship of the Director of Human Resources.

1. Original application and accompanying documents related to the hiring process such as resumes and transcripts.
2. Change of address and personnel action notices of pay and status changes.
3. Performance appraisals and related materials.
4. Tuition reimbursement documentation.
5. Employee history updating information submitted by employees including recent education, records of outside achievements, changes affecting withholding tax, etc.

Policy No.: 204
Page 2 of 2

PERSONNEL RECORDS & PRIVACY, continued

6. Documents necessary for the administration of the company benefit programs.

7. References from previous employers, medical records, and any investigatory information will be kept in a separate, confidential file. This file may be examined only by appropriate officials conducting an investigation.

Personnel records will be retained for five years beyond an employee's separation date.

B. *Access to Personnel Files:*

Files may be examined by supervisors and department heads on a "need to know" basis.

Employees may examine their own files at reasonable times and upon request submitted to the Human Resources Department. This review will take place in the personnel records area.

C. *References and Release of Information:*

If employees wish the company to verify information requested by outside sources for credit or other purposes, they must first sign a release of information form (copy attached).

If former employees wish us to provide an employment reference, we will do so but only with their written authorization. All requests for references should be referred to the Human Resources Department.

EXERCISE #3: (continued)

XYLON COMPANY

Authorization to Release Information

I hereby authorize the release of the information indicated below regarding my employment at Xylon Company.

- ☐ Any information requested.
- ☐ Salary history.
- ☐ Dates of employment.
- ☐ Positions held.
- ☐ Duties and responsibilities.
- ☐ Prospect for continued employment.
- ☐ Reason for leaving.

_____   _____
                    Signature   Date

Name: _____

Social Security # _____

XYLON COMPANY

Subject: **PERFORMANCE APPRAISAL**	Policy No.: 603 Page 1 of 2 Date: May 21, 19XX

I. PURPOSE

To provide a process by which the job performance of each employee is appraised for the purposes of development, merit review, and counselling.

II. POLICY

The employee performance appraisal process accomplishes the following objectives:

A. Provides employees with full information concerning their performance.

B. Identifies performance elements in which employees do well and those in which they require improvement, and to establish plans to correct performance deficiencies.

C. Provides a basis for linking employee performance to merit increases in salary.

III. PROCEDURES

Each supervisor will conduct performance appraisals for each subordinate employee.

A. *Timing:*
   1. All regular full-time employees will receive at least one appraisal during a calendar year on their anniversary date.
   2. For newly hired employees, a special appraisal and review will occur each month to the end of their introductory period, three months later, and annually thereafter.
   3. The Human Resources Department will maintain a system assist supervisors in completing performance appraisals timely.

EXERCISE #3: (continued)

Policy No.: 603.
page 2 of 2

B. *Performance Appraisal Form:* A copy of the Employee Performance Appraisal form and a copy of the Introductory Performance Evaluation form is attached.

C. *Performance Appraisal Discussion:* Supervisors will hold individual discussions with each employee regarding performance. These discussions should be held at a pre-arranged time in a private location free from interruptions. Each employee will be asked to review and sign the performance appraisal form.

Key elements for supervisors in the appraisal process are:

1. Review performance on each of the evaluation factors on the appraisal form. Performance strengths as well as deficiencies should be covered to let employees know that you are aware of good performance as well as of that which needs improvement.

2. Review in detail plans to improve performance during the next period.

3. Make every effort to involve the employee in the discussion. Gaining agreement and commitment to improve goals, even modest ones, improves the likelihood that positive change will result.

SUGGESTED SOLUTIONS FOR EXERCISE #3

1. Overtime Pay

Suggested Solution: Non-exempt employees will be paid time and one-half their regular rate of pay for authorized hours worked in excess of forty in one week and eight in one day.

All overtime work by non-exempt employees must be authorized in advance by the responsible supervisor or department head.

2. Personnel Records

Suggested Solution: Important events in your history with the company will be recorded and kept in your personnel file. Annual performance reviews, change of status records, commendations, and educational attainment records are examples of records maintained.

You will receive a copy of any record initiated by the company. Also your personnel file is available for your inspection in the Human Resources Department. Contact your supervisor to make an appointment.

3. Performance Appraisals

Suggested Solution: You will receive a performance appraisal from your supervisor once a month to the end of your 90-day Introductory Period. Thereafter, appraisals will be scheduled near your employment anniversary date. The performance appraisal is a vehicle for you and your supervisor to discuss your general performance. It will cover your strengths as well as ways in which you may be able to improve. It is also an opportunity for you to discuss your job concerns and career development goals.

> If your responses differ from the suggestions above, remember that there is more than one way to write a good policy summary. Just make sure that yours is complete, clear, and concise.

TESTING AND VERIFYING
THE CONTENTS

After you've selected the topics and drafted the text, test how well employees understand it before you send your manual to the printer.

You can do this with a focus group—a small group of employees who will help you determine how effective your HR Manual is.

FOCUS GROUPS

1. Select five to seven employees who are verbal and forthright. Be sure to choose a cross-section of people (that is, people from different departments and at different levels in the company). A cross-section of people helps ensure that employees from all levels and all departments will understand and better appreciate the HR Manual.

2. Distribute the HR Manual draft to the group and ask each member to read it carefully and evaluate it.

3. Schedule a one or two hour follow-up meeting for the next week.

4. During the meeting, in an informal and open discussion, encourage observations and comments from all members of the group. Write agreed upon comments on a chalkboard or flip chart.

5. At the end of the meeting, note your conclusions and incorporate the group's unanimous suggestions into the final revision of the manual.

ONE LAST CHECK

Now give the final draft to your company's attorney to make sure its contents and wording are appropriate from a legal perspective.

By setting up a focus group to test the manual and by getting the approval of your attorney, you'll be more secure that your document is clear, complete, and legally correct.

PART 4

USING YOUR HUMAN RESOURCES MANUAL

YOU CAN DO IT!

USING YOUR HUMAN RESOURCES MANUAL

Since you'll spend considerable time preparing your manual and ensuring the contents are complete and accurate, we've included a few suggestions to help you use it more effectively.

1. Distribute it to every employee, and make sure new employees receive a copy as part of their orientation. Have them sign a Receipt of Handbook and put it into their personnel files.

2. Tack a copy of the HR Manual on the employee bulletin board to ensure it's readily accessible to all employees.

3. Include a suggestion form as the last page in the manual to encourage comments or suggestions for improvements and additions.

4. Review your manual annually; update, if necessary, to include changes in the law and useful suggestions from your employees.

5. If you decide there are sufficient or significant enough changes to merit a reprint, distribute the new handbooks to every employee. If you choose not to reprint, make sure written statements of new rules, regulations, or policies are distributed to employees and posted on company bulletin boards.

PART 5

REVIEW

CAN WE HELP YOU?

We know we've provided a lot of useful information, yet with HR Manuals it's difficult to cover everything. For example, we've mentioned the differences between an HR Manual and a Policy Manual. If you don't have a Policy Manual and are interested in developing one, or if you have questions or comments about something else we've mentioned, we'd like to hear from you. Please drop us a line at the address below, and we'll respond as soon as we can.

Sue Brock/Sally Cabbell
Writing a Human Resources Manual
c/o Crisp Publications, Inc.
95 First Street
Los Altos, CA 94022

SUMMARY OF WORKSTEPS FOR WRITING A NEW HR MANUAL

1. Prepare a **checklist** of subjects you think should be included.

2. Prepare an **interview guide** to solicit information from supervisors and managers in your organization.

3. Interview managers and **outline** the results of your interviews.

4. Reformat the outline into a **Table of Contents.**

. . . . **You're half way home!** . . . .

5. Gather all the **written company policies** for each subject in your Table of Contents.

6. **Write a summary** of the detailed policy in first-party language for the HR Manual.

7. Write summaries of all subjects in the Table of Contents.

8. Write a brief Company history.

9. Have the president of your company write a **Welcome Letter** and philosophy statement.

10. Draft a **Suggestion Form** and a **Receipt of Manual** Form.

11. Design and draft the HR Manual's **cover.**

12. Assemble all draft materials into several **mock copies.**

13. **Test** the effectiveness of your Manual with a focus group you have organized.

14. **Revise** and submit the final draft to your attorney for review.

15. **Finalize** and **print.**

16. **Distribute,** take a deep breath, and relax. You've just completed a major project for your organization. You should be feeling a deep sense of satisfaction. As a matter of fact, we think **you deserve a day off!**

APPENDIX

A. Subjects to Consider: Mandatory, Important, and Nice-to-Have

B. Sample Table of Contents for a Policy Manual

C. Sample Table of Contents for an HR Manual

D. Sample HR Manual for Xylon Company

WELCOME TO THE XYLON CORPORATION

SUBJECTS TO CONSIDER: MANDATORY, IMPORTANT & NICE-TO-HAVE

Here is a long but not complete list of specific policies you'll want to refer to in addition to the checklist on page 10 as you select topics for your HR Manual. We've organized the following policies into three categories: Mandatory, Important, and Nice-To-Have. The mandatory policies involve federal regulations that apply to most employers.

Mandatory Policies:

Accidents
Affirmative Action
Disability
Drugfree Workplace
Complaints
Equal Employment Opportunity
Exempt/non-exempt classification
Harassment
Holidays
Hours of Work
Jury Duty
Leaves and Absences
- civic affairs
- disability
- military
- pregnancy

Military Reserve Training, Annual
Overtime Payment
Personnel Records
- privacy
- inspection
- release of information
- retention

Safety
Status, Definitions of Employment
Voting
Workers' Compensation

Important Policies

Attendance/Absenteeism/Lateness
Bereavement Leave
Change of Status
Communications
  bulletin boards
  handbooks
  opinion surveys
Confidential Information
Conflict of Interest
Discharge
Dress/Appearance
Employee Assistance Programs
Employment
  agreements
  approvals
  independent contractor

  minors
Exit Interview
Medical Records
Non-Union Employee Relations
Probationary Period
Performance Appraisal, Employee
Political Activities of Employees
Probationary Period, New Employee
Promotion
  job posting
  compensation
  wage/salary administration
Relocation of Employees
Severance Pay
Sick Leave
Termination

Nice-To-Have Policies

Address Change
Advance in Pay (Loans)
Automobiles
Awards
Bonding
Business Conference
Contributions/Collections
Counseling
Credit Union
Death of Employee
Demotion
Education, Aid to
Employee Services

Expenses
  air travel
  auto travel
  accommodations
  meal allowance
Flexible Work Schedule
Food Service
Garnishment
Gifts or Gratuities
Health & Welfare Plans
  life
  accidental death & dismemberment
  dental

NICE-TO-HAVE POLICIES (continued)

hospital/surgical/medical
major medical
vision care
long-term disability
prescription drug
travel accident
Housekeeping
Identification, Employee
Internal Assignment
Job Descriptions
Library
Lost and Found
Meal Allowance
Medical and Dental Appointments
Medical Approval
  return to work
  restrictions
  physical examination
  medical department
Memberships
Minors
Objectives, Company
Organizational Charts
Outside Employment
Parking
Passes
Patents
Personal Time Off
Policy and Procedure Manual

Profit Sharing
Purchases, Employee
Radios
Recognition, Employee
Recreation, Activities
Recruiting/Hiring
  rehire
  orientation of new employees
  relatives
  physical examination
  sabbatical
Retirement Plan
Salary Continuation Plan
Savings Bonds
Separation
Service Awards
Smoking
Social Security
Solicitations
Suggestion Plan
Telephones
Training and Development
Transfer
Travel Insurance
Tuition Aid
Unemployment Compensation Tax
Uniforms
Union Relations
Visitors/Tours

SAMPLE TABLE OF CONTENTS FOR A POLICY MANUAL

XYLON COMPANY POLICY MANUAL

CONTENTS

100. **HIRING/SEPARATION**

    101. Definitions of Employment Status
    102. Recruiting and Selection

        102.1 Acceptable Pre-employment Inquiries Under EEO Guidelines

    103. Equal Employment Opportunity
    104. Introductory Period for New Employees

        104.1 Introductory Period for Sales Representatives

    107. Severance Pay
    108. Exit Interviews

200. **WAGE & SALARY ADMINISTRATION**

    201. Wage and Salary Program

        201.1 Position Description Questionnaire
        201.2 Exempt/Non-exempt Classification

    202. Overtime: Non-exempt Employees
    203. Hours of Work and Paydays
    204. Personnel Records and Privacy

300. **EMPLOYEE BENEFITS AND SERVICES**

    301. Vacations
    302. Holidays
    303. Sick Leave
    304. Leaves of Absence
    305. Bereavement Leave
    306. Jury Duty and Court Appearance
    307. Military Reserve Training Leave
    308. Time Off for Voting

    350. Profit Sharing

    370. Employee Facilities and Services

SAMPLE TABLE OF CONTENTS FOR A COMPANY POLICY MANUAL (continued)

XYLON COMPANY POLICY MANUAL (continued)

400. GENERAL PERSONNEL POLICIES

- 401. Conflict of Interest
- 402. Use of Company Telephones
- 404. Standards of Conduct

    404.1 Guidelines in Administering Progressive Discipline

- 405. Smoking in the Workplace
- 406. Attendance Control

    406.1 Guidelines in Administering Attendance Control

500. COMMUNICATIONS

- 501. Employee Handbook
- 502. Complaint Handling
- 503. Non-Union Employee Relations

600. EMPLOYEE TRAINING AND DEVELOPMENT

- 601. Employee Orientation and Training
- 602. Tuition Reimbursement
- 603. Performance Appraisal
- 604. Promotions

700. SAFETY & HEALTH

- 701. Accidents; Emergency Reporting
- 720. Safety Shoes: Warehouse Personnel

800. LAWS AND REGULATIONS DEALING WITH PERSONNEL

Listing of Relevant Laws and Regulations

900. MANAGEMENT POLICY MEMOS

INDEX

JOB DESCRIPTIONS

SAMPLE TABLE OF CONTENTS FOR TWO HR MANUALS

Montgomery Bank
Employee Handbook

Contents

Benefits: A Summary 1

Health and Dental Care 15

General Information 16
Health Maintenance Organizations 25
Health Plan 61
Alcohol and Drug Abuse Plan 68
Dental Plan 76

Disability Income 81

Sick Pay 82
Disability Income—California 83
Disability Income—Other States 90
Long Term Disability Plan (LTD) 92

Life and Accident Plans 97

Life Insurance Plans 97
Personal Accident Insurance 101
Travel Accident Insurance 105

Investment Plans 107

Tax Advantage Plan 108
Employee Stock Ownership Plan 127
Employee Stock Purchase Plan 132

The Retirement Plan 137

Separation Pay Plan 157

Standards of Business Conduct 161

Conflicts of Interest 162
Confidential and Proprietary
  Information 168
Personal Finance 170
Responsibilities 172

You and Your Job 175

How We're Organized 175
Equal Employment and
  Affirmative Action 176
Our Employment Relationship 178
You and Your Supervisor 178
Your Personnel Officer 178
Your Work Schedule 179
How You Are Paid 180
Your Salary 183
Performance Planning and Review 188
Career Development 190
Time Off 194
Leaves of Absence 198
Grievance Resolution 201
Infoline 202
Employee Assistance Services 202
Safety Program 203
Volunteer Network 203
Some Responsibilities to
  Montgomery 204
More Programs and Services 207
Personnel Files 209
Background Checks 210
Termination 210
Retiree Status Eligibility 211

*Appendix A: Benefit Plans Administration
  and Appeals* 213

*Appendix B: ZIP Codes Covered
  by HMOs* 221

Index 235

56

SAMPLE TABLE OF CONTENTS FOR TWO HR MANUALS (continued)

YOU AND KRISP   Human Resources Manual

Code of Personnel Relations 3
The Company and You...planning for your career 5
How You Are Paid...pay for performance 15
The Krisp Health Care Program...guarding your family's health.
    Basic Health Care Plan 20
    Health Maintenance Organizations 38
    Extended Health Care Plan 41
    Krisp Medical Assistance Plan 54
    Dental Assistance Plan 77
The Elective Benefit Account...ways to save on taxes 86
The Krisp Retirement Income Plan...for peace of mind
                      in your retirement years 103
The Krisp Family Protection Program...financial security for
                      you and yours 115
Income Protection Plans...
  when you must be away from work.
    Short-Term Disability Plan 126
    Long-Term Disability Plan 132
    Personal Absence Policy 138
    Other Absences 140
    Termination Allowance Plan 142
Wage Dividend...
  for your part in the company's success 147
Investment Plans...for a financially secure future.
    Savings and Investment Plan 148
    Tax Credit Stock Ownership Plan 160
    Other Investment Opportunities 164
Leisure Time...helping you get away from it all.
    Holiday Plan 166
    Vacation Plan 168
General Information...additional plan details.
    Claims and Appeal Procedures 172
    Your Rights Under ERISA 174
    Health Care Contributions 175
    Coordination of Benefits 175
    Continuation of Health Care Coverage 177
    Plan Modification and Termination 178
    Plan Documents 178
Your Anniversaries...benefits milestones in your career 179
Index 180

XYLON COMPANY
HUMAN RESOURCES MANUAL

(Here is the HR Manual as it appears in XYLON COMPANY'S Policy Manual)

Subject:
  Employee Handbook

Policy #501
Page 1 of 1
Date: February 21, 19XX

XYLON
EMPLOYEE HANDBOOK

I. PURPOSE

To explain to all employees their benefits, opportunities, and responsibilities while employed by the company.

II. POLICY

Each employee will be given an Employee Handbook at the time of employment. The handbook includes summaries of key policies, procedures, benefits, and standards governing employment at Xylon Company. Employees will be asked to read it carefully, and acknowledge in writing that they have received it and understand it.

XYLON COMPANY

Welcome to Xylon Company. In 1973, I began with three, part-time employees, using a two-car garage as our warehouse.

Today, we are a growing corporation, recognized as one of the finest marketing and distributing organizations in the industry.

I feel our success can be attributed to team work, dedication, professionalism, and our employees. You are our company's most valuable asset.

If you have any concerns regarding your employment with the company, I or any member of management would be happy to help you.

I wish you success and good luck with your career at Xylon Company.

Sincerely,

Roger Stephens

B. Roger Stephens
President

BRS/cb

XYLON COMPANY
EMPLOYEE HANDBOOK

XYLON COMPANY
EMPLOYEE HANDBOOK

September, 19XX

This handbook has been prepared to introduce you to our company and acquaint you with the policies, rules, pay, and benefits which apply to your employment here.

Please read this handbook carefully and keep it handy for future reference. One of your first responsibilities is to become familiar with its contents and to review it with your supervisor or the Human Resources Department if you have any questions.

EMPLOYMENT POLICIES

Equal Opportunity

Xylon Company maintains a policy of nondiscrimination with all employees and applicants for employment. All aspects of employment with us are governed on the basis of merit, competence, and qualifications and will not be influenced in any manner by race, color, religion, sex, age, national origin, handicap, or veteran status.

All decisions made with respect to recruiting, hiring, and promoting for all job classifications will be made solely on the basis of individual qualifications related to the requirements of the position. Likewise, the administration of all other personnel matters such as compensation, benefits, transfers, education, and social/recreation programs will be free from any illegal discriminatory practices.

Definitions of Employment Status

The following terms will be used to describe the classification of employees and their employment status:

Exempt

Employees whose positions meet specific tests established by the Fair Labor Standards Act (FLSA) and are exempt from overtime pay requirements.

Non-exempt

Employees whose positions do not meet FLSA exemption tests and are paid one and one-half times their regular rate of pay for hours worked in excess of 8 per day and forty per week.

XYLON EMPLOYEE HANDBOOK

Full-Time Page 2

Employees who work an average of at least 30 hours per week on a regular basis. Full-time employees are eligible for all benefits when applicable service requirements are met.

Part-Time

Employees scheduled to work an average week of fewer than 30 hours. They are not eligible for company benefits.

Introductory

New employees, other than sales representatives, with fewer than 90 days of service.

Regular

Full-time employees who have completed the 90-day introductory period. They are employed for an indefinite length of time and eligible for all employee benefits.

Introductory Period for New Employees

The introductory period for new employees lasts up to 90 days from date of hire. During this time, you have your first opportunity to evaluate Xylon Company as a place to work, and we have our first opportunity to evaluate you as an employee.

This period involves special orientation activities plus closer and more frequent performance evaluations than that given to regular employees. Sales representatives have an introductory period specially tailored to their job requirements.

Upon satisfactory completion of the introductory period, you will become a regular employee. All employees, regardless of classification, status, or length of service, are expected to meet and maintain company standards for job performance and behavior.

Personnel Records

Important events in your history with the company will be recorded and kept in your personnel file. Annual performance reviews, change of status records, commendations, and educational attainment records are examples of records maintained.

You will receive a copy of any record initiated by the company. Also, your personnel file is available for your inspection in the Human Resources Department. Contact your supervisor to make an appointment.

XYLON EMPLOYEE HANDBOOK

General Policy

We strive to maintain rates of pay at Xylon Company that are comparable or superior to those of other companies in our industry or in the San Francisco Bay Area with similar kinds of work.

Our wage and salary plan classifies each position on the basis of:
- Knowledge and ability requirements.
- Variety and scope of responsibilities.
- Physical and mental demands.

Established wage or salary ranges are reviewed once per year and adjusted as necessary. If you are interested in knowing the wage and salary range for your position, ask your supervisor.

Overtime Pay

Non-exempt employees will be paid time and one-half their regular rate of pay for authorized hours worked in excess of forty in one week and eight in one day.

All overtime work by non-exempt employees must be authorized in advance by the responsible supervisor or department head.

Hours of Work

For most employees our normal work week consists of 37-1/2 hours, worked 7-1/2 hours per day, 8:00 a.m. to 4:00 p.m., Monday through Friday. Warehouse hours are from 7:00 a.m. to 4:00 p.m. The warehouse will be closed from 12:00 noon to 1:00 p.m. If your position is in the warehouse, your supervisor will discuss this with you in more detail.

Paydays

Paydays are on the 15th and the last working day of each month. If the 15th falls on a holiday or weekend, you will be paid on the preceding workday.

Employment of Minors

As a general rule, regular employees of the company must be 18 years of age or older. Occasionally, we hire students or others who are 16 or 17 years old, but this is done only under special conditions and must be approved in advance by the Human Resources Department.

Lunch and Rest Periods

The lunch period for most employees is one-half hour. Each department schedules two, ten minute breaks per day, one in the morning and one in the afternoon. All of these periods are important for your rest and well-being. It is also important that they not be abused.

XYLON EMPLOYEE HANDBOOK

EMPLOYEE BENEFITS AND SERVICES

Xylon Company offers a comprehensive package of group insurance and other benefit programs for its employees. Complete and official details of our group insurances are contained in plan documents included in your orientation materials or available through the Human Resources Department. Details of our other benefits and policies are contained in the Management Systems Manual available for your review through your supervisor. Some of these plans are summarized here to give you only highlights and to let you know that they are available. In each case, the official plan documents, trust agreements and policy statements will govern in the event of any conflict in the information presented. Please refer to the booklet "Health Protection Plan" for important details not covered here or see your supervisor.

Group Insurance

  Medical

  Cost: Company paid.

  Inpatient: Maximum benefit per confinement (Room and Board, Miscellaneous Services and Supplies). $2,500.00

  Outpatient: Surgery; emergency care of accidental injury; pre-admission testing. Paid as a Miscellaneous Service as above.

  Ambulance: $150.00 per trip

  Major Medical: Deductible: $100.00 per individual per year
  $300.00 per family per year

  Benefit: First $2,500.00 of eligible expenses - 50%

  Eligible expense over $2,500.00 - 100%

Dental

Cost: Company paid.

Deductible: $25.00 per calendar year per individual.

Benefit: Type A. Prosthetics (crowns, fixed bridgework, dentures) and gold restorations. 50%

  Type B. All other eligible dental services and supplies. 80%

Maximum Benefit: $1,000.00 per calendar year.

XYLON EMPLOYEE HANDBOOK

Life Insurance and Accidental Death and Dismemberment

Group term life insurance for each employee is provided in the amount of $5,000.00. If an employee dies from any cause, the insurance proceeds will be paid to his or her beneficiary in the designated manner, either installments or a lump sum.

Long-Term Disability

After 90 days of continuous disability, employees will receive 50% of their salary up to a maximum benefit of $2,000.00 per month for five years, if sick, or to age 65 if disabled. This insurance is company-paid.

Annual Physical Examination Allowance

The company will pay $100.00 per year toward the cost of a physical examination or GYN exam as a way of assisting employees with their own health maintenance program.

Pension and Profit-Sharing Plans

Pension Plan

Participation in the Pension Plan is at no cost to you. The company contributes an amount equal to 5% of annual compensation to fund the program. Once the eligibility requirement has been met, vesting in the program grows by 10% each year so that by the end of the 10th year of service you are fully vested in the Pension Plan. Eligibility commences on the May 1st following six months of continuous service.

Profit Sharing

Many employees have an opportunity to share in the company's success through participation in the Profit-Sharing Plan. Each fiscal year, 5% of pre-tax profits are set aside for distribution to eligible employees. The proportion of an individual's distribution is calculated by dividing that employee's annual base salary by the total annual base salary of all participants. To be eligible, you must have completed at least one full year of employment by April 30, be employed in a regular full-time status, and not be an executive or receive commissions as part of your compensation.

XYLON EMPLOYEE HANDBOOK

Benefits Mandated by Laws and Regulations

State Unemployment Insurance (SUI)

Xylon Company contributes to the State Unemployment Insurance Fund. No contribution is made by you. The purpose of this insurance is to protect you from a total loss of wages when you are unemployed through no fault of your own and assuming you are available, able, and actively seeking other employement. Since the amount paid by the company into this fund is affected by our experience rating, all aspects of this program are carefully monitored.

Social Security (FICA)

This federal program provides a base retirement income and other benefits for all eligible participants. It is financed both by employees and employers. The amount of required contribution depends upon a formula prescribed by law and subject to change.

Workers' Compensation

This insurance protects you against economic loss caused by work-related accidents or illnesses. The amount of benefits is determined by law on a case-by-case basis. The company pays the entire cost of the program, and coverage depends upon prompt reporting of accidents/illnesses and filing claims.

California State Disability Insurance (SDI)

This plan will provide benefits to offset income loss due to illness or disability that is not work-related. Generally, you are eligible for benefits after the first day of hospital confinement or the 8th day of a disability that prevents you from working. The plan is financed entirely by employee contributions so be sure to apply for the benefits when eligible. We will be glad to help you with this.

66

XYLON EMPLOYEE HANDBOOK

Page 7

Time Off and Excused Absences

Vacations

Our vacation plan is designed to provide you with the opportunity to rest and get away from the everyday routine. Your entitlement:

Length of Service Completed	Vacation Time Earned
1 through 4 years	10 working days
5 through 9 years	15 working days
10 years or more	20 working days

Vacations must be taken during the 12 months immediately following your anniversary date and must be scheduled in advance with your supervisor. In order to satisfy your preferences as well as meet the staffing needs of the department, discuss your vacation plans well in advance with your supervisor and complete a Request for Vacation form as required.

Vacations may not be accumulated from year to year and no pay-in-lieu of vacation time will be authorized except upon termination.

Holidays

Full-time employees are eligible for nine paid holidays in each calendar year. They are:

New Year's Day	Thanksgiving Day
President's Day	Friday following Thanksgiving
Memorial Day	Christmas Eve
Independence Day	Christmas Day
Labor Day	

When a company holiday falls on Sunday, the following Monday will be observed as the holiday. If a holiday falls on Saturday, the preceding Friday will be observed as the holiday.

Sick Leave

After completing the 90-day Introductory Period you will be eligible for three days of sick-leave time. Thereafter, you will accumulate one day of additional sick-leave eligibility for each completed full calendar month of service.

Total eligibility may accumulate from year to year to a maximum of 60 days. During sick leave, your regular salary will be continued (offset by any Workers' Compensation or State Disability benefits you receive), but there will be no pay for unused days at the end of a year or upon termination.

XYLON EMPLOYEE HANDBOOK

Bereavement Leave

In the event of death in your immediate family, you may have up to three days off, with pay, to handle family affairs and attend the funeral. "Immediate family" is defined as: father, mother, brother, sister, spouse, child, mother-in-law, father-in-law, grandparents, and grandchildren.

Jury Duty

In order that you may serve on a jury without loss of earnings, the company will pay the difference between your regular earnings and the fee you receive for jury service for up to 10 working days per calendar year. Additional time will be considered a Leave of Absence without pay. Please contact your supervisor promptly after receiving notification to appear for potential jury service.

Leaves of Absence Without Pay

Leaves of absence without pay may be granted to regular, full-time employees in order to maintain continuity of service in instances where unusual or unavoidable circumstances require prolonged absence.

Leaves of Absence without pay are of the following types:

Disability Leave

Up to 120 days in the case of illness or disability when supported by a physician's statement. Accrued Sick Leave benefits must be used before commencement of this leave.

Maternity Leave

Same as Disability Leave.

Emergency Personal Leave

From 30 to 60 days may be granted for compelling personal reasons. Requires one year of service and the approval of your supervisor. Approval is based on department work requirements, among other factors.

Military Service Leave

For the duration of required service.

Military Reserve Training

Required initial training plus up to two weeks per year. At your option, this training may be combined with paid vacation time.

There are other important considerations including benefit coverage while on leave and reinstatement procedures. Please see your supervisor well in advance to discuss these and other matters.

EMPLOYEE DEVELOPMENT

Performance Appraisals

You will receive a performance appraisal from your supervisor at the end of your 90-day introductory period and again six months later. Thereafter, appraisals will be scheduled near your employment anniversary date. The performance appraisal is a vehicle for your supervisor to discuss your general performance. It will cover your strengths as well as ways in which you may be able to improve. It is also an opportunity for you to discuss your job concerns and career development goals.

Tuition Reimbursement

We would like to encourage you to improve your education and skills. Under special circumstances, employees may be reimbursed for the tuition cost of educational courses taken outside normal working hours. Should you desire to participate in such a program, consult with Human Resources for details of the policy and for a Tuition Reimbursement form.

COMPANY RULES AND STANDARDS OF CONDUCT

Groups of people who are working together for any purpose require certain guidelines pertaining to their conduct and relationships. Accordingly, it is important that all of us be aware of their responsibilities to the company and to fellow employees.

It is our intention to take a constructive approach in this area and at the same time insure that actions which would interfere with our operations or an employee's job are not continued.

Not conforming to our standards will result in one of the following forms of disciplinary action: verbal warning, written warning, decision leave, or discharge. In arriving at a proper course of action, the seriousness of the infraction, past record of the employee, and circumstances surrounding the matter will be considered.

XYLON EMPLOYEE HANDBOOK

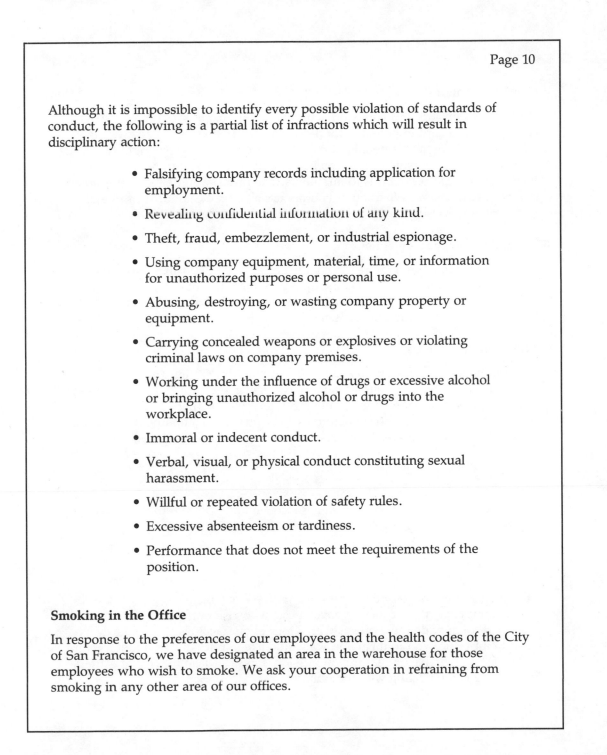

Page 10

Although it is impossible to identify every possible violation of standards of conduct, the following is a partial list of infractions which will result in disciplinary action:

- Falsifying company records including application for employment.

- Revealing confidential information of any kind.

- Theft, fraud, embezzlement, or industrial espionage.

- Using company equipment, material, time, or information for unauthorized purposes or personal use.

- Abusing, destroying, or wasting company property or equipment.

- Carrying concealed weapons or explosives or violating criminal laws on company premises.

- Working under the influence of drugs or excessive alcohol or bringing unauthorized alcohol or drugs into the workplace.

- Immoral or indecent conduct.

- Verbal, visual, or physical conduct constituting sexual harassment.

- Willful or repeated violation of safety rules.

- Excessive absenteeism or tardiness.

- Performance that does not meet the requirements of the position.

Smoking in the Office

In response to the preferences of our employees and the health codes of the City of San Francisco, we have designated an area in the warehouse for those employees who wish to smoke. We ask your cooperation in refraining from smoking in any other area of our offices.

XYLON EMPLOYEE HANDBOOK

Conflict of Interest

Due to the demands and competitive nature of our business, we have a special concern with regard to potential conflict of interest that arises mostly through additional employment (moonlighting). While we recognize your right to engage in other activities outside of your job here, we do expect you to devote your full working time and best efforts to our affairs. The primary guideline in this area is one of full disclosure. We ask that you discuss all possible conflicts of interest with your supervisor.

Using the Company Telephone

Telephone facilities are required to conduct our company business during working hours. Circumstances come up occasionally where it is necessary to make or receive personal telephone calls during business hours but they should be limited in both length and frequency.

Attendance Standards

Top production is necessary to keep all departments operating smoothly. It is essential, therefore, that your attendance be regular and punctual. If you must be absent from work due to illness or other reasons, we ask that you notify your supervisor or department head before work begins. The company phone number is (805) 771-9000. When reporting your absence, please try to give your expected date of return.

Absence Without Notice

After three consecutive days of absence without notice to the company an employee will be presumed to have voluntarily quit and will be separated from the payroll.

Appearance

All our employees are asked to dress in a professional, business-like, and well-groomed manner. We frequently have guests who visit our offices and it is customary to provide these guests with a tour of our facilities. We make every effort to introduce you to them and we would like to put our "best foot forward" and create a favorable and lasting impression. Physical cleanliness is of extreme importance when dealing with the public.

XYLON EMPLOYEE HANDBOOK

COMMUNICATIONS

Resolving Employee Complaints

Under normal conditions, if you have a job-related problem, question, or complaint, you should discuss it with your supervisor. The simplest, quickest, and most satisfactory solution often will be reached at this level.

If the discussion with your supervisor does not answer your question or resolve the matter to your satisfaction within two or three days, you may then present your case to the manager of your department or the Director, Human Resources. At this point, if the matter is still not resolved satisfactorily, you may present your case in writing to the President who will investigate it and make the final decision.

Difficulties in using this complaint procedure should be brought to the attention of the Director, Human Resources.

Non-union Employee Relations

There are no unions at Xylon Company. We believe that our employee relations programs and policies make unions unnecessary, and we intend to make every legal effort to keep it that way. We have a good working environment with customers and employees and our relationships are free of artificially created tensions that could be brought on by outside parties. Xylon Company was built from the ground up by Roger Stephens and a hard-working group of employees who designed policies and programs in a sincere effort to provide fair treatment for all. We are continuing that philosophy today.

XYLON EMPLOYEE HANDBOOK

EMPLOYEE SAFETY AND HEALTH

We make every effort to provide safe working conditions for our employees. We observe the safety laws of the governmental bodies within whose jurisdiction we operate. No one will knowingly be required to work in any unsafe manner. Safety is every employee's responsibility. Therefore, all employees are requested to point out potential hazards and do everything reasonable to keep the company a safe place to work.

In line with this policy, we require that safety shoes be worn by those who regularly work in the warehouse. Safety shoes are those which offer foot protection from pallets or falling objects and which in themselves do not create a hazard of tripping or falling.

Accidents

If an injury occurs on the job, no matter how slight, report it immediately to your supervisor or department head. Failure to report an injury could affect a subsequent Workers' Compensation claim.

First Aid

Two first aid kits are located in strategic areas, one in the office of the Director, Human Resources, and one in the warehouse break area. These contain standard supplies of band-aids, merthiolate, burn ointment, antiseptic spray, gauze, adhesive tape, eye wash, triangular bandages, gauze pads, and aspirin. Not all items are included in each of the kits, so be certain to check both for medical supplies.

If a first aid situation exists and you are not certain how to handle it, ask the receptionist to call for help immediately.

General Emergencies

Fire is an ever-present hazard, especially where electrical equipment is concerned. Familiarize yourself with the fire extinguisher locations and the building exits. This information will be pointed out to you during your orientation, but it is a good practice to review this information periodically. Every employee should know where the extinguishers are located and how to operate them effectively.

Since we live in an area where earthquakes occur, employees should be aware of their surroundings within the office, and will be rehearsed in procedures to follow during and after an earthquake. These training sessions will be conducted periodically as needed. Specifics of the plan are maintained in your supervisor's policy manual and are available for your inspection.

XYLON EMPLOYEE HANDBOOK

Page 14

CHANGES IN POLICY

The policies contained in this employee handbook may be changed when, in the opinion of management, circumstances require it. While it is our intention to provide you with advance notice of any changes, it may not always be possible. Therefore, don't consider this to be a fixed contract. Stay in close communication with your supervisor to be sure you are up to date and recognize that changes in policy are management's prerogative.

INDEX

A

Absence Without Notice, 12
Accidental Death and
   Dismemberment Insurance, 5
Accidents, Reporting, 13
Annual Physical Exam Allowance, 5
Appearance Standards, 12
Appraisals, Performance, 9
Attendance Standards, 12

B

Benefits, Employee, 4
Bereavement Leave, 8

C

Changes in Policy, 14
Complaints, Resolving, 12
Conflict of Interest, 11

D

Dental Insurance, 5
Disability Insurance, 5
Disability Leave, 8
Disability, Long Term, 5

E

Emergencies, General, 14
Emergency Leave, 8
Employee Purchases, 9
Employee Relations, Non-Union, 13
Equal Employment Opportunity, 1
Exempt, Employment Status, 1

F

Full-time Employment Status, 2
First Aid, 13

G

H

Health and Safety, 13
Health, Medical Insurance, 4
Holidays, 7
Hours of Work, 3

I

Inspection of Personnel File, 2
Introductory Employment Status, 1
Introductory Period for New
   Employees, 2

J

Jury Duty, 8

K

L

Leaves of Absence, 8
Life Insurance, 5
Lunch Period, 4
Lunchroom, 9

XYLON EMPLOYEE HANDBOOK

INDEX, Continued

M

Major Medical Insurance, 4
Maternity Leave, 8
Medical Insurance, 4
Military Leave, 8
Minors, Employment of, 3

N

Non-exempt Employment Status, 1
Non-union Employee Relations, 13

O

Overtime Pay, Non-exempt
   Employees, 3

P

Part-time Employment Status, 2
Paydays, 3
Pension Plan, 5
Performance Appraisals, 9
Personal Leave Emergency, 8
Personnel Records, 2
Physical Examination, 5
Policies, Changes, 14
Profit Sharing Plan, 5

Q

R

Regular Employment Status, 2
Reserve Training, Military, 8
Rest Periods, 4
Rules, Company, 10

S

Safety and Health, 13
Safety Shoes, 13
Seminars, Wine, 9
Sick Leave, 7
Smoking in the Office, 11
Social Security, 6
Standards of Conduct, 10
State Disability Insurance, 6
State Unemployment Insurance, 6

T

Tastings, Wine, 9
Telephone, Use of, 11
Tuition Reimbursement, 10

U

Unemployment Insurance, State, 6

V

W

Wage and Salary Policies, 3
Workers' Compensation, 6

X

Y

Z

NOTES

FOR OTHER FIFTY-MINUTE SELF-STUDY BOOKS
SEE ORDER FORM AT THE BACK OF THE BOOK.

NOTES

FOR OTHER FIFTY-MINUTE SELF-STUDY BOOKS
SEE ORDER FORM AT THE BACK OF THE BOOK.

NOTES

FOR OTHER FIFTY-MINUTE SELF-STUDY BOOKS
SEE ORDER FORM AT THE BACK OF THE BOOK.

NOTES

ABOUT THE FIFTY-MINUTE SERIES

''Every so often an idea emerges that is so simple and appealing, people wonder why it didn't come along sooner. The Fifty-Minute series is just such an idea. Excellent!''

Mahaliah Levine, Vice President for
Training and Development
Dean Witter Reynolds, Inc.

WHAT IS A FIFTY-MINUTE BOOK?
—Fifty-Minute books are brief, soft-covered, ''self-study'' titles covering a wide variety of topics pertaining to business and self-improvement. They are reasonably priced, ideal for formal training, excellent for self-study and perfect for remote location training.

''A Fifty-Minute book gives the reader fundamentals that can be applied on the job, even before attending a formal class''

Lynn Baker, Manager of Training
Fleming Corporation

WHY ARE FIFTY-MINUTE BOOKS UNIQUE?
—Because of their format. Designed to be ''read with a pencil,'' the basics of a subject can be quickly grasped and applied through a series of hands-on activities, exercises and cases.

''Fifty-Minute books are the best new publishing idea in years. They are clear, practical, concise and affordable—perfect for today's world.''

Leo Hauser, Past President
ASTD

HOW MANY FIFTY-MINUTE BOOKS ARE THERE?
—Those listed on the following pages at this time. Additional titles are always in development. For more information write to **Crisp Publications, Inc.,** **95 First Street, Los Altos, CA 94022.**

THE FIFTY-MINUTE SERIES

Quantity	Title	Code #	Price	Amount
	MANAGEMENT TRAINING			
	Successful Negotiation	09-2	$7.95	
	Personal Performance Contracts	12-2	$7.95	
	Team Building	16-5	$7.95	
	Effective Meeting Skills	33-5	$7.95	
	An Honest Day's Work	39-4	$7.95	
	Managing Disagreement Constructively	41-6	$7.95	
	Training Managers To Train	43-2	$7.95	
	The Fifty-Minute Supervisor	58-0	$7.95	
	Leadership Skills For Women	62-9	$7.95	
	Systematic Problem Solving & Decision Making	63-7	$7.95	
	Coaching & Counseling	68-8	$7.95	
	Ethics in Business	69-6	$7.95	
	Understanding Organizational Change	71-8	$7.95	
	Project Management	75-0	$7.95	
	Managing Organizational Change	80-7	$7.95	
	Working Together	85-8	$7.95	
	Financial Planning With Employee Benefits	90-4	$7.95	
	PERSONNEL TRAINING & HUMAN RESOURCE MANAGEMENT			
	Effective Performance Appraisals	11-4	$7.95	
	Quality Interviewing	13-0	$7.95	
	Personal Counseling	14-9	$7.95	
	Job Performance and Chemical Dependency	27-0	$7.95	
	New Employee Orientation	46-7	$7.95	
	Professional Excellence for Secretaries	52-1	$7.95	
	Guide To Affirmative Action	54-8	$7.95	
	Writing A Human Resource Manual	70-X	$7.95	
	COMMUNICATIONS			
	Effective Presentation Skills	24-6	$7.95	
	Better Business Writing	25-4	$7.95	
	The Business of Listening	34-3	$7.95	
	Writing Fitness	35-1	$7.95	
	The Art of Communicating	45-9	$7.95	
	Technical Presentation Skills	55-6	$7.95	
	Making Humor Work	61-0	$7.95	
	Visual Aids in Business	77-7	$7.95	
	Speed-Reading in Business	78-5	$7.95	
	Influencing Others: A Practical Guide	84-X	$7.95	
	SELF-MANAGEMENT			
	Balancing Home And Career	10-6	$7.95	
	Mental Fitness: A Guide to Emotional Health	15-7	$7.95	
	Personal Financial Fitness	20-3	$7.95	
	Attitude: Your Most Priceless Possession	21-1	$7.95	
	Personal Time Management	22-X	$7.95	

(Continued on next page)

THE FIFTY-MINUTE SERIES

Quantity	Title	Code #	Price	Amount
	SELF-MANAGEMENT (CONTINUED)			
	Preventing Job Burnout	23-8	$7.95	
	Successful Self-Management	26-2	$7.95	
	Developing Positive Assertiveness	38-6	$7.95	
	Time Management And The Telephone	53-X	$7.95	
	Memory Skills In Business	56-4	$7.95	
	Developing Self-Esteem	66-1	$7.95	
	Creativity In Business	67-X	$7.95	
	Managing Personal Change	74-2	$7.95	
	Winning At Human Relations	86-6	$7.95	
	Stop Procrastinating	88-2	$7.95	
	SALES TRAINING/QUALITY CUSTOMER SERVICE			
	Sales Training Basics	02-5	$7.95	
	Restaurant Server's Guide	08-4	$7.95	
	Quality Customer Service	17-3	$7.95	
	Telephone Courtesy And Customer Service	18-1	$7.95	
	Professional Selling	42-4	$7.95	
	Customer Satisfaction	57-2	$7.95	
	Telemarketing Basics	60-2	$7.95	
	Calming Upset Customers	65-3	$7.95	
	Quality At Work	72-6	$7.95	
	Managing A Quality Service Organization	83-1	$7.95	
	ENTREPRENEURSHIP			
	Marketing Your Consulting Or Professional Services	40-8	$7.95	
	Starting Your Small Business	84-0	$7.95	
	Publicity Power	2-3	$7.95	
	CAREER GUIDANCE & STUDY SKILLS	.05		
	Study Skills Strategies	07-X	$7.95	
	Career Discovery	48-6	$7.95	
	Plan B: Protecting Your Career From	59-9	$7.95	
	I Got The Job!		$7.95	
	OTHER CRI ning	00-9		
	Comfort Zones: A Practical Gu	11-8	$13.95	
	Stepping Up To Supervisor arents	19-X	$13.95	
	The Unfinished Business Of Living: H	23-7	$12.95	
	Managing Performance g	47-5	$18.95	
	Be True To Your Future: A G	49-1	$13.95	
	Up Your Productivity	79-1	$10.95	
	How To Succeed In	27-3	$7.95	
	Practical Time Management	5-4	$13.95	
	Copyediting: A Practical Guide	51-3	$18.95	

THE FI[barcode]RIES

☐ Send volume discount information.

☐ Please send me a catalog.

	Amount
Total (from other side)	
Shipping ($1.50 first book, $.50 per title thereafter)	
California Residents add 7% tax	
Total	

Ship to: _____

_____

_____

_____

Phone number: _____

Bill to: _____

_____

_____

_____

P.O. # _____

All orders except those with a P.O.# must be prepaid.
For more infor_____ Call (415) 949-4888 or FAX (415) 949-1610.

BU_____

FIRST _____

_____ ALTOS, CA

POSTAGE WILL BE PAID BY

Crisp Publication__
C__First Street
95__ Al__os, CA
Los __

NO POSTAGE
NECESSARY
IF MAILED
IN THE
UNITED STATES

ML,t